# Blessed Are the Music-Makers

# Blessed are the Music Makers

## Warm-ups for the Musician's Spirit

### Alan J. Hommerding

World Library Publications
the music and liturgy division of J. S. Paluch Company, Inc.
Schiller Park, Illinois

ISBN: 1-58459-198-6

WLP Customer Care: 800 566-6150
Toll-free Fax: 888 957-3291
wlpcs@jspaluch.com
www.wlpmusic.com

# Table of Contents

## Easter

## Days of Proclamation

## Ministry Occasions

# Foreword

Music directors are constantly preparing—choosing music, creating programs, attending meetings, and conducting rehearsals. Members of choirs and other musical ensembles likewise discover at a very early stage that they will be spending far more time engaged in rehearsals and in other preparation activities than in singing or playing at actual liturgical celebrations.

While all of these preparatory activities are important, even essential, surely common prayer is every bit as necessary as warming up the voice or tuning an instrument. Praying together roots us and unites us. Prayer provides the foundation for carrying out our ministry as a response to a call from God. Praying in common prepares us to minister together as one choir or ensemble as we join and lead the entire assembly in a communal act of worship.

One of the main reasons that many parish members choose to participate in liturgical music ministry is to help themselves and others enter into the liturgy at a deeper level. The prayers in this book will help them to do just that. Alan Hommerding has provided liturgically based prayers for music ministers to use as they prepare for worship or for other occasions when they gather together. He has drawn on his deep knowledge and love of the liturgy to craft prayer experiences that will draw musicians into the spirit of the various Sundays and seasons.

These prayers have deep roots in the Word of God that is proclaimed in the liturgical assembly. Like the psalms, canticles, hymns, and anthems that directors choose for the liturgy, the texts in this book lead participants to pray with images from Scripture: living water, vine and branches, light and darkness. The prayers found here also make frequent references to the scripture readings that are proclaimed during the various seasons of the liturgical year. In this way, they help to form musicians into people who pray the scriptures according to the rhythm of the church year. This formation is vital, since psalmists, cantors, choirs, and other musicians are so frequently entrusted with proclaiming sung texts from the Bible as they carry out their ministry.

Another important contribution of this collection is the inclusion of a sung litany for each set of prayer texts. If music ministers are to lead assemblies in singing the liturgy—rather than punctuating a recited liturgy with songs—then they themselves need to be formed in the art and practice of sung prayer. In addition to praying with psalms and hymns at their gatherings, musicians will benefit greatly from singing these simple intercessory prayer settings as they prepare for worship.

Directors who find themselves scrambling for appropriate prayer suggestions for various events will be grateful to find here prayers for a concert or tour, and on the occasion of the departure or death of a member of the music ministry.

In this collection, Alan Hommerding has provided music ministers with an extraordinarily rich and valuable resource for their common prayer. May all who use this book be formed into more committed servants of the worshiping assembly and of the liturgy itself.

J. Michael McMahon, President
National Association of Pastoral Musicians
Feast of Our Lady of Guadalupe
December 12, 2003

# Suggestions for Use

*Blessed Are the Music-Makers: Warm-ups for the Musician's Spirit* is intended for use by choirs and other music ministry ensembles at rehearsals, prior to worship, or at any gathering of musicians.

Prayers for the Sundays and seasons of the year have been approached in a two-fold manner. The liturgical seasons with a consistent number of Sundays or celebrations from year to year (Advent, Christmas, Lent, Easter) have prayers provided for each Sunday or feast. The sections "Days of Discipleship" and "Days of Proclamation" encompass the remainder of the year. "Days of Discipleship" are intended for those Sundays between the close of the Christmas season and the beginning of Lent, when the focus of the Lectionary Gospels is on the call of the disciples and the early public ministry of Jesus. "Days of Proclamation" are for the Sundays following Pentecost, arranged according to various topics, as we hear scriptures about the Church living out its mission in the Spirit.

Each Sunday or feast includes the following types of prayers:

**Litany** — All the litanies are provided with a short response and four invocations (along with the option for another invocation for particular needs). These may be sung or recited. Communities that sing a seasonal or common psalm response at worship may wish to use that response or another simple liturgical response. For those who prefer beginning rehearsal with song, an easy chanting tone is provided for the individual invocations of the litany. These tones may need to be adapted or transposed if other responses are used. More adventurous prayer leaders may improvise their own tones for these prayers. Litany invocations may be led by the director, a cantor, or any member of the ensemble able to do so. If sung, it is recommended that they be *a cappella*. If the litany is used as a closing prayer, an additional invocation, such as "For what else shall we pray?", may be used to allow members of the group to voice their own needs.

**Gathering Prayer** — This is a scripture-based prayer, led by one member of the group. After the invitation "Let us pray," the leader should allow some time for silent prayer. The concluding formula always follows the same pattern in order to enable the concluding "Amen" from the entire group.

**Brief Gathering Prayer** — For occasions when a brief prayer is desired (the end of rehearsal or prior to Sunday worship, for example), this shorter prayer has been provided. The concluding formula, again, follows the same pattern to enable "Amen" by all.

**Suggested Scriptures** — For those groups who wish to begin rehearsal with a brief reading from scripture, several suggestions have been provided. Other appropriate scripture passages may be chosen by the prayer leader.

Prayers for special music ministry occasions and feasts are provided as well.

These are only initial suggestions for the use of this resource. They may be varied and used in different ways throughout a music group's ministry. Adaptation and creativity in their use will make this resource more fruitful for the prayer of those who make music for the glory of God.

Alan J. Hommerding

# ADVENT AND CHRISTMAS

# Advent I
# Prepare the Way

## Litany

R. Come, O Lord; come set us free.    *(tone for intercessions)* we pray:

*(A seasonal psalm refrain or another seasonal response may be used.)*

For the grace to call upon the name of God,
    so we might remain ever-faithful, we pray: R.

That the Lord will find us ready, doing what is right,
    repenting what **is** not, we pray: R.

That we will look forward eagerly to the day of fulfillment,
    promised by **the** Lord, we pray: R.

For ears to hear the herald voice, eyes to see signs of glory,
    watchful, **a**wake, we pray: R.

*(If desired, an additional invocation for particular needs may be added.)*

## Gathering Prayer

*Leader:* Let us pray. *(Pause for silent prayer.)*

Shepherd of Israel,
in love you grant us this season of Advent,
a new dawn of grace to begin our celebration,
our reflection upon your saving power in Jesus Christ.
As we come together, may we make music in the Spirit.
Grant us your light, keep us steadfast,
guide our growth in love through prayer and song.
We ask this of you, our one, true, living God,
forever and ever. Amen.

## Brief Gathering Prayer

*Leader:* Let us pray.

God, redeemer forever,
thank you for the grace bestowed on us in Christ.
May our ministry prepare the hearts of all
as we wait for you to come in glory.
We pray in the one voice of the Spirit,
one God forever and ever. Amen.

## Suggested Scriptures

Jeremiah 33:14–16
Romans 13:11–12
Mark 13:33–37

Alan J. Hommerding
Text and music © 2004, World Library Publications

# Advent II
# A Voice Cries Out

## Litany

℟. Come, O Lord; come set us free.  *(tone for intercessions)* we pray:

*(A seasonal psalm refrain or another seasonal response may be used.)*

For the desire to follow the example of the Baptist's her**ald** voice, we pray: ℟.

That our ministry may bring God's comfort to those who have **no** hope,
  we pray: ℟.

For the building of communities and nations that live
  and believe **in** harmony, we pray: ℟.

That we may always sing of God's peaceful kingdom,
  where jus**tice** reigns, we pray: ℟.

*(If desired, an additional invocation for particular needs may be added.)*

## Gathering Prayer

*Leader:* Let us pray. *(Pause for silent prayer.)*

Let your Spirit rest upon us, God, our hope;
may we answer the call to sing praises to your name,
here and among all the nations.
Shake off our mourning and misery,
fill our mouths with laughter, place your joy on our lips.
Join our voices to the voice of the Baptist,
proclaiming a new heaven and new earth in Christ,
who lives and reigns with you,
one God forever and ever. Amen.

## Brief Gathering Prayer

*Leader:* Let us pray.

Our voices sing out in expectation, saving God.
You have begun your work in us;
complete it on the day of Christ's coming.
*"Marana tha!"* "Come, Lord!"
Today, forever and ever. Amen.

## Suggested Scriptures

Baruch 5:1–4
Romans 15:5–6
Luke 3:4–6

Alan J. Hommerding
Text and music © 2004, World Library Publications

# Advent III
# Wait for the Lord

## Litany

℟. Come, O Lord; come set us free.     *(tone for intercessions)* we pray:

*(A seasonal psalm refrain or another seasonal response may be used.)*

That our joyful hearts will lead us onward in song
   to the house of **the** Lord, we pray: ℟.

That we may be known as witnesses to the Light **from** Light, we pray: ℟.

For our troubled world, for the gift of peace
   that surpasses all un**der**standing, we pray: ℟.

For an eager, patient yearning as we wait for the heavens
   to rain down **the** Just One, we pray: ℟.

*(If desired, an additional invocation for particular needs may be added.)*

## Gathering Prayer

*Leader:* Let us pray. *(Pause for silent prayer.)*

Faithful God who calls us,
send your Spirit upon us
so that we may delight in you.
May your Spirit in us never be quenched.
Let the joyful news of your Son's coming
resound through our music.
Make us messengers sent ahead of him,
proclaiming repentance and rejoicing.
Hear us, answer us, come to us, Lord,
now and forever. Amen.

## Brief Gathering Prayer

*Leader:* Let us pray.

Lord, we hear you say, "Be strong, fear not."
Let us proclaim these mighty words, hearts filled with hope,
preaching your good news,
forever and ever. Amen.

## Suggested Scriptures

Isaiah 35:10
Philippians 4:4–7
Matthew 11:2–6

Alan J. Hommerding
Text and music © 2004, World Library Publications

# Advent IV
# Annunciations

## Litany

℟. Come, O Lord; come set us free.　*(tone for intercessions)* we pray:

*(A seasonal psalm refrain or another seasonal response may be used.)*

That God will strengthen and cheer us in the gospel of Je**sus** Christ,
　　we pray: ℟.

For the courage of Joseph to be dreamers who hear and follow **God's** voice,
　　we pray: ℟.

For the bold obedience of Mary, that we might bear the Word of God
　　in our **low**liness, we pray: ℟.

That the King of Glory will enter our lives,
　　making us living temples of **the** Spirit, we pray: ℟.

*(If desired, an additional invocation for particular needs may be added.)*

## Gathering Prayer

*Leader:* Let us pray. *(Pause for silent prayer.)*

God-among-us,
our joyful Advent journey
has brought us nearer to the day of your coming;
keep us one in mind, heart, and faith
with the herald voices of your messengers.
May we strive to hear your angels
and echo their song to your glory.
Be our peace, our Emmanuel,
now and forever. Amen.

## Brief Gathering Prayer

*Leader:* Let us pray.

Your name is majesty, O God!
Forever we sing your goodness;
let us also seek to do your will,
hearing and believing in your word,
now and forever. Amen.

## Suggested Scriptures

Micah 5:3–4
Romans 16:25–27
Matthew 1:23–24

Alan J. Hommerding
Text and music © 2004, World Library Publications

# Christmas I
# The Birth of Christ

## Litany

℟. Glo - ri - a in ex - cel - sis De - o! *(tone for intercessions)* we pray:

*or*

℟. Glo - ry to God in the high - est! *(tone for intercessions)* we pray:

*(A seasonal psalm refrain or another seasonal response may be used.)*

That the joy of this season will cause our new song to resound
to the ends of the **earth**, we pray: ℟.

For the knowledge that the Lord delights in us,
and a generous heart to share that delight with **all**, we pray: ℟.

That we might seek the wonder of God's glory in the poor and **lowly**,
we pray: ℟.

For the wisdom to worship Christ with all of God's **angels**, we pray: ℟.

*(If desired, an additional invocation for particular needs may be added.)*

## Gathering Prayer

*Leader:* Let us pray. *(Pause for silent prayer.)*

God of endless glory,
Christ, our Savior, is born today!
We bow before the wonder of this mystery:
your love humbly born, so we may walk in your light
and dwell in darkness no more.
We reflect on the glory of this day;
through the power of your Spirit we sing your song,
ever-new in Christ,
forever and ever. Amen.

## Brief Gathering Prayer

*Leader:* Let us pray.

God Most High, your promise is fulfilled
in the fruit of Jesse's tree and David's royal house:
Christ, our Lord and Savior,
forever and ever. Amen.

## Suggested Scriptures

Isaiah 9:5–6
Hebrews 1:5–6
Luke 2:10–14

Alan J. Hommerding
Text and music © 2004, World Library Publications

# Christmas II
# The Word of God in Flesh

## Litany

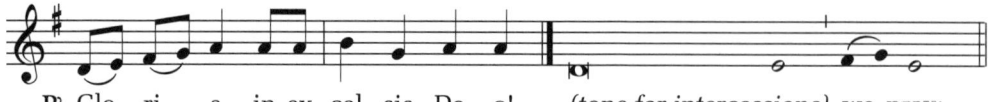

R̸. Glo - ri - a  in ex- cel- sis  De - o!     *(tone for intercessions)* we pray:

*or*

R̸. Glo - ry to God in the  high - est!     *(tone for intercessions)* we pray:

*(A seasonal psalm refrain or another seasonal response may be used.)*

For joyful hearts and voices, a new song in Christ who dwells a**mong us**,
    we pray: R̸.

That the wonder of this season will lead us to be witnesses
    to the dawn of heaven's **grace**, we pray: R̸.

For those who listen in silence to hear the angels sing God's grace upon **grace**,
    we pray: R̸.

That we may be messengers of the Holy One each day,
    bringing glad tidings of sal**vation**, we pray: R̸.

*(If desired, an additional invocation for particular needs may be added.)*

## Gathering Prayer

*Leader:* Let us pray. *(Pause for silent prayer.)*

Eternal God,
your infinite Word embraced our human flesh,
born in our nakedness to one day die in nakedness,
gently swaddled, as if tenderly wrapped in a shroud.
Through the gift of your Holy Spirit,
we see your love revealed to us today.
May we sing in endless wonder and praise
to your boundless glory,
forever and ever. Amen.

## Brief Gathering Prayer

*Leader:* Let us pray.

Ever-living God, today is born light, joy, and peace.
From the dawn of our days you spoke to redeem us;
in Christ is your glory
forever and ever. Amen.

## Suggested Scriptures

Isaiah 52:7–8
Titus 2:11–12
John 1:1–5

Alan J. Hommerding
Text and music © 2004, World Library Publications

# Christmas III
# The Holy Family

## Litany

R̸. Glo - ri - a in ex - cel - sis De - o!   *(tone for intercessions)* we pray:

*or*

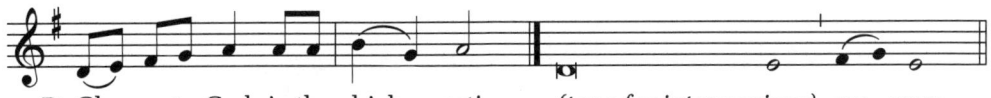

R̸. Glo - ry to God in the high - est!   *(tone for intercessions)* we pray:

*(A seasonal psalm refrain or another seasonal response may be used.)*

That the joy and glory of this season will ring out in psalms, hymns,
   and inspired **songs**, we pray: R̸.

For a greater desire to honor all peoples of the world,
   raising up God's house of **justice**, we pray: R̸.

That we will live as God's chosen ones: holy, compassionate, kind,
   humble, gentle, and **patient**, we pray: R̸.

For the strength to heed the voice of Christ until the day we are called
   to his Father's **house**, we pray: R̸.

*(If desired, an additional invocation for particular needs may be added.)*

## Gathering Prayer

*Leader:* Let us pray. *(Pause for silent prayer.)*

Trinity most blessed,
in the love of Joseph, Mary, and Jesus
we see a reflection of your own perfect love.
Bind us together in the word of Christ,
your divine Word made incarnate in our human family.
Watch over every household of faith;
hear the prayer of your daughters and sons
who sing your glory
now and forever. Amen.

## Brief Gathering Prayer

*Leader:* Let us pray.

God of Promise, may we continue to walk in your ways,
dedicated to you in these days of your Son's Nativity.
Hold your faithful children in loving-kindness,
now and forever. Amen.

## Suggested Scriptures

Genesis 15:5–6
Colossians 3:16–17
Luke 2:49–52

Alan J. Hommerding
Text and music © 2004, World Library Publications

# Christmas IV
# The Epiphany

**Litany**

R̸. Glo - ri - a   in ex- cel- sis  De - o!     *(tone for intercessions)* we pray:

*or*

R̸. Glo - ry to God  in the  high - est!     *(tone for intercessions)* we pray:

*(A seasonal psalm refrain or another seasonal response may be used.)*

For the wisdom to journey in the light of heaven,
   so we may come to find the **Christ**, we pray: R̸.

That we will be wise stewards of God's grace,
   offering to others every gift bestowed on **us**, we pray: R̸.

For every nation on earth: may all come to flower with justice,
   living in profound **peace**, we pray: R̸.

That our share in the splendid hymn of angels and starlight
   will make us **radiant**, we pray: R̸.

*(If desired, an additional invocation for particular needs may be added.)*

## Gathering Prayer

*Leader:* Let us pray. *(Pause for silent prayer.)*

God of every nation,
your light and peace appear today in Christ.
Let your glory shine on us and fill us;
lead us to sing joyfully of this wondrous mystery.
Make us wise so that we may seek you
among the poor, afflicted, and lowly.
We offer you the gift of our lives,
bowed down in worship before you,
now and forever. Amen.

## Brief Gathering Prayer

*Leader:* Let us pray.

Shine on us in glory, Creator of the stars;
guide our footsteps to Christ our Morningstar,
your profound peace singing in our hearts
now and forever. Amen.

## Suggested Scriptures

Isaiah 60:1–3
Ephesians 3:2–3
Matthew 2:10–11

Alan J. Hommerding
Text and music © 2004, World Library Publications

# Christmas V
# The Baptism of the Lord_____

## Litany

R̂. Glo - ri - a in ex - cel - sis De - o! *(tone for intercessions)* we pray:

*or*

R̂. Glo - ry to God in the high - est! *(tone for intercessions)* we pray:

*(A seasonal psalm refrain or another seasonal response may be used.)*

For all the baptized, the Church, born anew in water and Spirit,
 beloved children of **God**, we pray: R̂.

For the Sun of Justice to shine forth from our lives each day,
 that all might sing "**Glory!**" we pray: R̂.

That we will be true servants, pleasing to the Lord,
 serving all who await **teaching**, we pray: R̂.

That our tongues will be loosened and livened by the voice
 that thundered over creation's **waters**, we pray: R̂.

*(If desired, an additional invocation for particular needs may be added.)*

## Gathering Prayer

*Leader:* Let us pray. *(Pause for silent prayer.)*

Peace to your people on earth,
God of all blessing.
Your Son began his mission in the waters of baptism;
keep us faithful to our baptismal call
to open eyes, to free prisoners,
always to proclaim the one mightier than we.
Pour out your spirit upon us once again,
so we may sing of your glorious reign,
now and forever. Amen.

## Brief Gathering Prayer

*Leader:* Let us pray.

We thank you, God of all creation,
for choosing us in baptism to be your children.
Send your Spirit to renew and guide us,
forever and ever. Amen.

## Suggested Scriptures

Isaiah 42:1–2
Acts 10:37–38
Mark 1:9–11

Alan J. Hommerding
Text and music © 2004, World Library Publications

# Christmas VI
# The Presentation of the Lord_____

## Litany

R̷. Glo - ri - a in ex - cel - sis De - o!  *(tone for intercessions)* we pray:

*or*

R̷. Glo - ry to God in the high - est!  *(tone for intercessions)* we pray:

*(A seasonal psalm refrain or another seasonal response may be used.)*

That our ministry will draw all people closer in Christ,
  who shared the fullness of our hu**manity**, we pray: R̷.

As the heavens raise their portals, may our hearts and voices
  be lifted in **music**, we pray: R̷.

That we may be strengthened and comforted by faith in the gospel
  when sorrow pierces our **hearts**, we pray: R̷.

That the light of grace shine in the world,
  guiding us in the ways of **holiness**, we pray: R̷.

*(If desired, an additional invocation for particular needs may be added.)*

## Gathering Prayer

*Leader:* Let us pray. *(Pause for silent prayer.)*

Strong and mighty God,
in human flesh you became one of us;
you call us sisters and brothers.
Lead us in the Spirit to your temple;
enfold us in the arms of your prophets
as we make music to your name, King of Glory.
In peace, may we one day see the gates of paradise
lifted up in your splendor,
forever and ever. Amen.

## Brief Gathering Prayer

*Leader:* Let us pray.

King of glory, Light of the world,
bring us in joy to the light of your temple.
Send us forth as your messengers,
now and forever. Amen.

## Suggested Scriptures

Malachi 3:1–2
Hebrews 2:14–15
Luke 2:29–32

Alan J. Hommerding
Text and music © 2004, World Library Publications

# DAYS OF DISCIPLESHIP

# Days of Discipleship
# The Call

## Litany

R. Hear us, O God; Call us to fol-low you.   *(tone for intercessions)* we pray:

*(A seasonal psalm refrain or another seasonal response may be used.)*

For attentive ears, hearts, and minds, ready to hear the voice of Christ:
   "Come, follow **me**!" we pray: R.

That we will consecrate our lives to discipleship,
   spreading the Good News in **music**, we pray: R.

For a courageous "Here am I!" and the readiness to leave behind
   all that keeps us from following Christ in **mission**, we pray: R.

Holy Spirit, source of every gift, let us seek your unity
   with those who share our **ministry**, we pray: R.

*(If desired, an additional invocation for particular needs may be added.)*

## Gathering Prayer

*Leader:* Let us pray. *(Pause for silent prayer.)*

Your voice, God of Glory,
resounded on the waters of our baptism;
let us hear that voice reverberate
in the call of Christ: "Follow me!"
May we be born anew for discipleship,
strong to make the Good News known
in music, in silence, in the unity that is yours,
one God forever and ever. Amen.

## Brief Gathering Prayer

*Leader:* Let us pray.

Lord God, send your Christ to walk among us
as on the shores of Galilee.
We pray to know and hear his voice calling to us.
Let us, in love and humble service, follow him,
forever and ever. Amen.

## Suggested Scriptures

Isaiah 49:1–3
1 Corinthians 12:4–6
Mark 1:14–15

Alan J. Hommerding
Text and music © 2004, World Library Publications

# Days of Discipleship
# Behold the Lamb of God

## Litany

℟. Hear us, O God; Call us to fol - low you.    *(tone for intercessions)*  we pray:

*(A seasonal psalm refrain or another seasonal response may be used.)*

Like John the Baptist, may our mission be to cry, "Behold!"
    and make known the splendor of the Lamb of **God**, we pray: ℟.

With the prophet Isaiah, may our tongues not be silent,
    may our mouths proclaim the glory of the **Lord**, we pray: ℟.

For the humility to seek the will of God so we may announce
    the kingdom of justice, joy, and **peace**, we pray: ℟.

Let the Word of the Lord, our Spirit and life, resound from our hearts,
    hands, and **voices**, we pray: ℟.

*(If desired, an additional invocation for particular needs may be added.)*

## Gathering Prayer

*Leader:* Let us pray. *(Pause for silent prayer.)*

God of our salvation,
you sent your only Son
to be our Paschal Lamb.
We sing of the saving mystery—
his life, passion, death, and resurrection—
so that we might grow closer to you
and draw nearer to one another in Christ,
in the unity of the Holy Spirit, forever and ever. Amen.

## Brief Gathering Prayer

*Leader:* Let us pray.

"Behold!" The Lamb takes away the sin of the world.
"Behold!" We are joyous witnesses of this Good News,
singing in God's saving power,
now and forever and ever. Amen.

## Suggested Scriptures

Isaiah 62:1–2
1 Corinthians 1:10–11
John 1:29–30

Alan J. Hommerding
Text and music © 2004, World Library Publications

# Days of Discipleship
# The Spirit Is upon Me

## Litany

R︮. Hear us, O God; Call us to fol - low you.     *(tone for intercessions)* we pray:

*(A seasonal psalm refrain or another seasonal response may be used.)*

That the glad tidings of scripture will always be fulfilled
   in our **ministry**, we pray: R︮.

For our loving and harmonious witness, may we never be a noisy gong
   or clanging **cymbal**, we pray: R︮.

May our music serve the Church's work for justice, charity, liberation,
   and **peace**, we pray: R︮.

That all we sing, say, or do will be offered to share the Good News
   of **salvation**, we pray: R︮.

*(If desired, an additional invocation for particular needs may be added.)*

## Gathering Prayer

*Leader:* Let us pray. *(Pause for silent prayer.)*

We sing of your salvation, Lord,
through your Spirit upon us today.
Make us servants of your faithful people,
joyful in our glad tidings
and steadfast in loving kindness.
Let your word be fulfilled
in our hearing and doing
today, every day, forever and ever. Amen.

## Brief Gathering Prayer

*Leader:* Let us pray.

Let the Spirit of your glad tidings
be upon us, O God.
Send us forth to proclaim your word,
so it might be fulfilled
in faithful discipleship to Christ,
now and forever. Amen.

## Suggested Scriptures

Jeremiah 1:4–5
1 Corinthians 2:1–3
Luke 4:14–15

Alan J. Hommerding
Text and music © 2004, World Library Publications

# Days of Discipleship
# Blessed Are You

## Litany

℞. Hear us, O God; Call us to fol - low you.　*(tone for intercessions)*　we pray:

*(A seasonal psalm refrain or another seasonal response may be used.)*

That our music-making will be a blessing and sign of God,
　wellspring of all **blessing**, we pray: ℞.

For the grace to find God's strength in our weakness,
　wisdom in our **foolishness**, we pray: ℞.

May the joy of God's song and the power of our witness
　shine for the world to **see**, we pray: ℞.

For the Spirit of jubilant praise to fill us always,
　even in times of **trial**, we pray: ℞.

*(If desired, an additional invocation for particular needs may be added.)*

## Gathering Prayer

*Leader:* Let us pray. *(Pause for silent prayer.)*

Font of all wisdom and blessing,
we bless you in our music-making
and we receive your blessing.
Our voices are raised in melody
to announce from on high
the light of your wondrous reign,
where weak are strong, foolish are wise,
and you call us "blessed"
forever and ever. Amen.

## Brief Gathering Prayer

*Leader:* Let us pray.

We bless you, Lord, source of every blessing.
Make us herald messengers of your reign
in our music-making,
bring us to your holy mountain,
to live with you forever and ever. Amen.

## Suggested Scriptures

Isaiah 58:7–8
1 Corinthians 1:27–28
Matthew 5:10–12

Alan J. Hommerding
Text and music © 2004, World Library Publications

# Days of Discipleship
# Signs and Wonders

## Litany

R̶. Keep us faith-ful, Lord;   and  hear  our  prayer.   *(tone for intercessions)*  we  pray:

*(A seasonal psalm refrain or another seasonal response may be used.)*

For the glory of the Lord to be revealed in the sign and symbol of **our** song,
  we pray: R̶.

May we savor the wedding feast of the Lamb as our song joins
  the prayers of heaven **and** earth, we pray: R̶.

For the ears of Cana's servants; may we hear the mother of Christ bid us,
  "Do as **he** tells you." we pray: R̶.

That the presence of God-among-us, Emmanuel, will fill us with thanks,
  praise, **and** worship, we pray: R̶.

*(If desired, an additional invocation for particular needs may be added.)*

## Gathering Prayer

*Leader:* Let us pray. *(Pause for silent prayer.)*

God of glory and wonder,
your presence in Christ is revealed
by the guiding light of a star,
by your voice and Spirit over the Jordan,
by transforming the waters of earth
into the everlasting wine of heaven.
We sing Christ our Morningstar, your Son, true Vine,
who lives and reigns with you,
one God, forever and ever. Amen.

## Brief Gathering Prayer

*Leader:* Let us pray.

God whose will is done on earth and in heaven,
help us listen for the voice of Christ so we may do as he tells us.
Keep us devoted in our ministry to your people,
now and forever. Amen.

## Suggested Scriptures

Daniel 2:20–22
Hebrews 2:2–4
John 2:3–5

Alan J. Hommerding
Text and music © 2004, World Library Publications

# Days of Discipleship
# Come unto Me

## Litany

℞. Keep us faith-ful, Lord; and hear our prayer. *(tone for intercessions)* we pray:

*(A seasonal psalm refrain or another seasonal response may be used.)*

That the voice of Christ in our music-making will ease the burdens
 of those **who** hear us, we pray: ℞.

For our ministry; may we serve in humility
 the least of the kingdom **of** God, we pray: ℞.

That the Holy Spirit of Good News and New Life will dwell in us
 and lead **our** witness, we pray: ℞.

Let our faith increase, so the Lord will live and work mighty deeds
 in **our** midst, we pray: ℞.

*(If desired, an additional invocation for particular needs may be added.)*

## Gathering Prayer

*Leader:* Let us pray. *(Pause for silent prayer.)*

God of the lowly, God of the mighty,
reveal your Son to us once again.
Let us be open to the sound of his call,
so his own voice may be on our lips in song.
May we desire only to lead others to Christ,
so our burdens may be lightened,
our infirmities healed, our divisions reconciled.
Increase our faith in you, our only God,
forever and ever. Amen.

## Brief Gathering Prayer

*Leader:* Let us pray.

Eternal is your word in our flesh, O God,
Christ Jesus the Lord.
We follow Christ, our burdens lightened, strengthened to serve you,
the One who calls us to sing of the kingdom,
now and forever. Amen.

## Suggested Scriptures

Jeremiah 31:23–25
1 John 5:1–3
Matthew 11:28–30

Alan J. Hommerding
Text and music © 2004, World Library Publications

# Days of Discipleship
# In Times of Trial

## Litany

℟. Keep us faith-ful, Lord;   and hear our prayer.   *(tone for intercessions)*   we pray:

*(A seasonal psalm refrain or another seasonal response may be used.)*

That we may be strong in the Lord, rejoicing when we are afflicted
    or in **distress**, we pray: ℟.

For all of us, temples of the Spirit, whose song is written not in ink
    but by **the** Spirit, we pray: ℟.

That we will always recall the love of the Lord, who loves us
    as a mother loves **her** child, we pray: ℟.

For the will, the desire, and the grace to love and pray for **our** enemies,
    we pray: ℟.

*(If desired, an additional invocation for particular needs may be added.)*

## Gathering Prayer

*Leader:* Let us pray. *(Pause for silent prayer.)*

God our comfort and consolation,
bless us with your presence today.
Remain with us in the struggles of life
and continue to strengthen us to serve.
Let our song of rejoicing go on;
may our witness to the gospel never waver
when we face trials or suffering.
Send your angels to watch over us,
forever and ever. Amen.

## Brief Gathering Prayer

*Leader:* Let us pray.

Loving God, in Christ you show us your caring presence,
staying with him through trials, suffering, and even death;
reassure us in our pain, bring us to a new song of joy,
now and forever. Amen.

## Suggested Scriptures

Isaiah 49:14–15
2 Corinthians 3:1–2
Luke 6:27–28

Alan J. Hommerding
Text and music © 2004, World Library Publications

# Days of Discipleship
# Be Forgiven, Be Healed

## Litany

℞. Keep us faith-ful, Lord; and hear our prayer. *(tone for intercessions)* we pray:

*(A seasonal psalm refrain or another seasonal response may be used.)*

May all who hear the Lord's song find balm for their wounds
and mercy for **their** souls, we pray: ℞.

That we will heed the call to be disciples of the healing, forgiving,
reconcil**ing** Christ, we pray: ℞.

By the power of resurrection, may every day be transformed
into a day holy to **the** Lord, we pray: ℞.

For all who suffer in spirit, mind, or body;
for households and friendships rent **a**sunder, we pray: ℞.

*(If desired, an additional invocation for particular needs may be added.)*

## Gathering Prayer

*Leader:* Let us pray. *(Pause for silent prayer.)*

Holy, holy, holy are you, Lord;
may your glory, which fills heaven,
fill the earth in the doing of your will.
Sanctify the music we make in your name;
let it be a messenger of mercy,
an ambassador of reconciliation,
a font of healing and restoration
in the Holy Spirit of Christ, your Son,
forever and ever. Amen.

## Brief Gathering Prayer

*Leader:* Let us pray.

Lord our God, you announced your kingdom in Christ;
may our music herald the mercy, forgiveness, and healing of his reign.
Make us stewards of your mysteries.
Hear and answer us now and forever. Amen.

## Suggested Scriptures

Isaiah 43:24–25
1 Corinthians 4:1–2
Matthew 9:12–13

Alan J. Hommerding
Text and music © 2004, World Library Publications

# Lent and Holy Week

# Ash Wednesday
# Return to the Gospel _____

## Litany

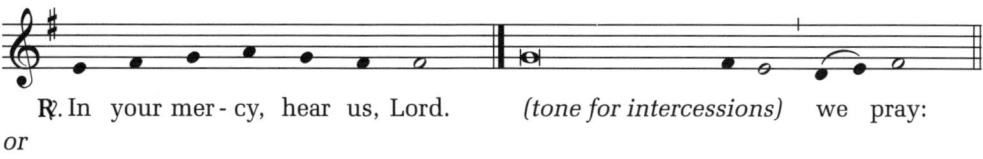

℞. In your mer-cy, hear us, Lord.    *(tone for intercessions)*    we pray:

or

℞. Ky-ri-e, e-le-i-son.    *(tone for intercessions)*    we pray:

*(A seasonal psalm refrain or another seasonal response may be used.)*

For the desire to reform our lives and return to **the** Gospel, we pray: ℞.

That our fasting will increase our hunger for justice, mercy, **and** peace,
    we pray: ℞.

That our prayer in song will renew us in the Spirit of baptis**mal** grace,
    we pray: ℞.

That our charity will make us wiser stewards of **our** gifts, we pray: ℞.

*(If desired, an additional invocation for particular needs may be added.)*

## Gathering Prayer

*Leader:* Let us pray. *(Pause for silent prayer.)*

Sound the trumpet blast, O Lord!
Lead us into this new time of grace.
Help us turn away from sin, hoping in your mercy.
Bring us back to the promise of the font,
where we were born anew as your children.
Grant us humility in all we do these forty days;
let all be done for your glory, not our own,
God of our salvation,
now and forever. Amen.

## Brief Gathering Prayer

*Leader:* Let us pray.

God of mercy, God of forgiveness,
be with us in this acceptable time.
May our song lead all hearts to repentance
and guide us toward Easter joy.
Make us ambassadors of reconciliation,
God Most Holy, God Most High,
forever and ever. Amen.

## Suggested Scriptures

Joel 12:15–16
2 Corinthians 5:20–21
Matthew 6:1–3

Alan J. Hommerding
Text and music © 2004, World Library Publications

# Lent I
# Trial and Temptation

## Litany

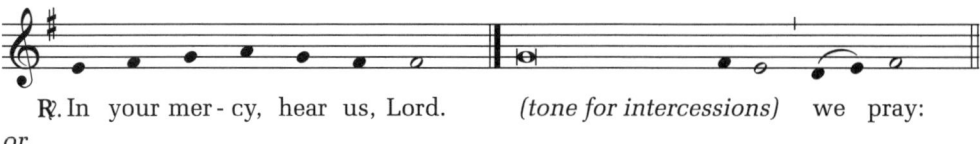

℟. In your mer-cy, hear us, Lord. *(tone for intercessions)* we pray:

*or*

℟. Ky-ri-e, e-le-i-son. *(tone for intercessions)* we pray:

*(A seasonal psalm refrain or another seasonal response may be used.)*

For hearts, minds, and tongues renewed in the grace of **the** Covenant,
 we pray: ℟.

That we may find life in every word that comes from the mouth **of** God,
 we pray: ℟.

For the strength of Christ, that we may endure when we face
 temptation **or** trial, we pray: ℟.

For those preparing to receive the Easter sacraments of light **and** life,
 we pray: ℟.

*(If desired, an additional invocation for particular needs may be added.)*

## Gathering Prayer

*Leader:* Let us pray. *(Pause for silent prayer.)*

Faithful, loving God,
lead us in the Spirit these Lenten days
to a renewed covenant with you,
our Creator and Redeemer.
With Christ we face the wilderness of evil;
in him we find your strong, tender hand.
Let us sing of your love and your truth, worshiping you alone,
forever and ever. Amen.

## Brief Gathering Prayer

*Leader:* Let us pray.

God our Creator,
you blew the breath of your Spirit into us
so we might sing of your salvation,
the Good News of Jesus Christ.
Make us strong and bold for this mission
these Lenten days, we pray to you,
now and forever. Amen.

## Suggested Scriptures

Genesis 9:8–11
Romans 5:12, 17
Mark 1:12–15

Alan J. Hommerding
Text and music © 2004, World Library Publications

# Lent II
# From Temptation to Transfiguration_____

## Litany

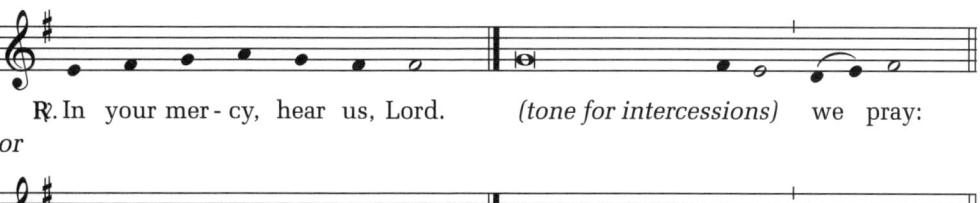

℟. In your mer - cy, hear us, Lord.     *(tone for intercessions)*     we pray:

*or*

℟. Ky - ri - e,   e - le - i - son.     *(tone for intercessions)*     we pray:

*(A seasonal psalm refrain or another seasonal response may be used.)*

For an ever-stronger faith, worthy of the children of Abraham **and** Sarah,
  we pray: ℟.

That we may live God's will on earth, and so receive a foretaste
  of the joyous choirs **of** heaven, we pray: ℟.

That we may be restored to the radiant light of bap**tismal** grace, we pray: ℟.

For those preparing to receive the Easter sacraments of light **and** life,
  we pray: ℟.

*(If desired, an additional invocation for particular needs may be added.)*

## Gathering Prayer

*Leader:* Let us pray. *(Pause for silent prayer.)*

Lord of Light Eternal,
speak to us from the bright cloud of your grace;
may we hearken in obedience to your voice,
as you call us your sons and daughters.
Keep us steadfast in prayer, fasting, and almsgiving;
bring us safely to the end of our Lenten journey.
Transform our ministry through the presence of your Spirit;
transfigure us by the power of resurrection,
now and forever. Amen.

## Brief Gathering Prayer

*Leader:* Let us pray.

God our light, God our salvation,
stay with us in this season of grace;
bring us through the discord of trial
to be transfigured by your song of glory.
Make us and keep us in your image,
the image of Christ,
forever and ever. Amen.

## Suggested Scriptures

Genesis 22:10–13
Romans 8:31–32
Mark 9:2–9

Alan J. Hommerding
Text and music © 2004, World Library Publications

# Lent III
# Living Waters of Grace_____

## Litany

℟. In your mer - cy, hear us, Lord.   *(tone for intercessions)*   we pray:

*or*

℟. Ky - ri - e, e - le - i - son.   *(tone for intercessions)*   we pray:

*(A seasonal psalm refrain or another seasonal response may be used.)*

For the living waters of grace to cleanse us **and** quench us, we pray: ℟.

That God will continue to guide our Lenten exodus to the promised **new** life, we pray: ℟.

For an increase in hope, poured into us through the Holy Spirit of **God's** love, we pray: ℟.

For those preparing to receive the Easter sacraments of light **and** life, we pray: ℟.

*(If desired, an additional invocation for particular needs may be added.)*

## Gathering Prayer

*Leader:* Let us pray. *(Pause for silent prayer.)*

God whose waters stream from the Temple,
cleanse us to be temples of your Spirit and truth,
lead us in fire and cloud, bring us safely through the sea
so we might sing a canticle of your praise.
Let the folly of the cross be our example,
Christ's desire to do your will be our wisdom.
In him you slake our thirst, so we never thirst again,
you, the God whom we worship,
now and forever. Amen.

## Brief Gathering Prayer

*Leader:* Let us pray.

Lord most kind and merciful,
you gave us your Son for eternal life.
The weakness of his cross is strength,
the water flowing from his side is life.
Keep us close to you in Spirit and truth,
forever and ever. Amen.

## Suggested Scriptures

Exodus 3:13–14
1 Corinthians 1:22–25
John 4:13–14

Alan J. Hommerding
Text and music © 2004, World Library Publications

# Lent IV
# Light for Our Eyes

## Litany

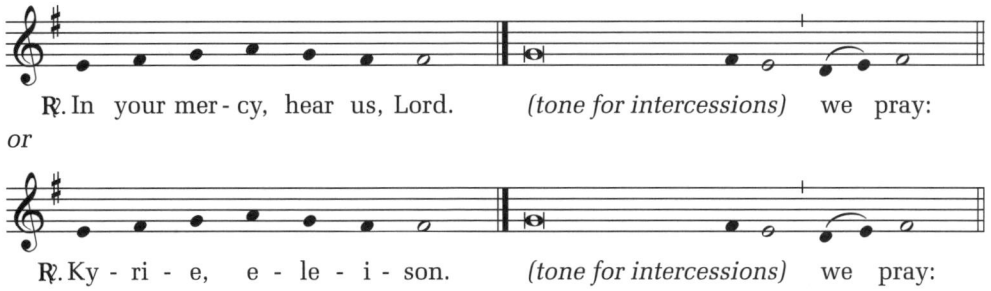

℟. In your mer-cy, hear us, Lord.    *(tone for intercessions)*    we pray:

*or*

℟. Ky-ri-e, e-le-i-son.    *(tone for intercessions)*    we pray:

*(A seasonal psalm refrain or another seasonal response may be used.)*

That our Lenten journey will be illuminated by the Light **from** Light,
    we pray: ℟.

For tongues that will sing the Lord's song, in ev**ery** place, we pray: ℟.

For ears always attentive for the Shep**herd's** voice, we pray: ℟.

For those preparing to receive the Easter sacraments of light **and** life,
    we pray: ℟.

*(If desired, an additional invocation for particular needs may be added.)*

## Gathering Prayer

*Leader:* Let us pray. *(Pause for silent prayer.)*

Lord, send your Spirit to rush upon us,
anoint us in baptism for the service of your people,
clothe us in light, make us children of light,
welcome us home with music and dancing.
The days of our Lenten wandering draw near their conclusion,
as you run to meet us once again
in the passion, death, and resurrection of Christ,
who lives and reigns with you and the Holy Spirit,
forever and ever. Amen.

## Brief Gathering Prayer

*Leader:* Let us pray.

With Lenten rejoicing we gather today,
God of life eternal,
this springtime of our song soon finding full flower
in the rising of Christ our Lord,
who lives and reigns forever and ever. Amen.

## Suggested Scriptures

2 Chronicles 36:15–16
Ephesians 5:8–10
John 3:16–18

Alan J. Hommerding
Text and music © 2004, World Library Publications

# Lent V
# The Resurrection and the Life_____

## Litany

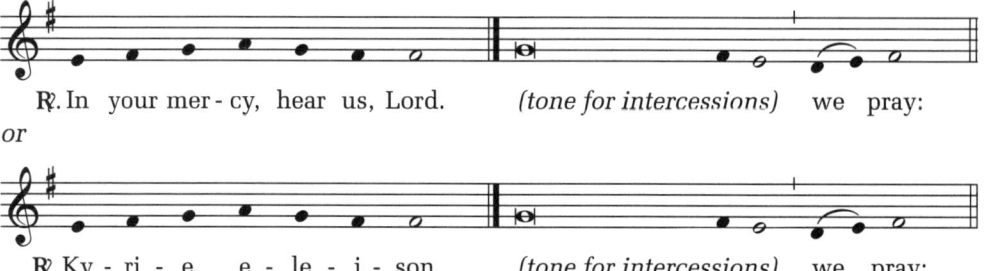

℟. In your mer-cy, hear us, Lord.  *(tone for intercessions)*  we pray:

*or*

℟. Ky-ri-e, e-le-i-son.  *(tone for intercessions)*  we pray:

*(A seasonal psalm refrain or another seasonal response may be used.)*

For the faith and hope to believe in Christ, our Resurrection **and** Life,
  we pray: ℟.

That we will always spread the gospel of the Liv**ing** Covenant, we pray: ℟.

For loving hearts ever open to forgive and **to** reconcile, we pray: ℟.

For those preparing to receive the Easter sacraments of light **and** life,
  we pray: ℟.

*(If desired, an additional invocation for particular needs may be added.)*

## Gathering Prayer

*Leader:* Let us pray. *(Pause for silent prayer.)*

Lord of Life, reach into our cold and stony hearts;
place your spirit of new life in us,
making us children and messengers of your new covenant,
written in the faithfulness of our ministry.
In the kindness and justice of our deeds,
may these last days of our exodus through Lent
return us again to you, as we celebrate the great mysteries
of Christ crucified, dead, buried, and risen to new life,
forever and ever. Amen.

## Brief Gathering Prayer

*Leader:* Let us pray.

Shatter our hearts of stone
with the music of your Word, Lord God.
bring us forth from our proud and unforgiving tombs,
and lead us to life eternal through Christ our Lord,
forever and ever. Amen.

## Suggested Scriptures

Ezekiel 37:12–14
Philippians 3:8–12
John 11:25–27

Alan J. Hommerding
Text and music © 2004, World Library Publications

# Palm Sunday
## Blessed Is He_____

### Litany

℟. In your mer-cy, hear us, Lord.    *(tone for intercessions)*    we pray:

*or*

℟. Ky-ri-e, e-le-i-son.    *(tone for intercessions)*    we pray:

*(A seasonal psalm refrain or another seasonal response may be used.)*

That we may willingly be Suffering Servants for the life of **the** world,
   we pray: ℟.

For the humility to follow Christ, obedient even unto death on **a** cross,
   we pray: ℟.

That we will always sing in faith: "Hosanna! Blessed is he who comes
   in name of **the** Lord!", we pray: ℟.

For those preparing to receive the Easter sacraments of light **and** life,
   we pray: ℟.

*(If desired, an additional invocation for particular needs may be added.)*

### Gathering Prayer

*Leader:* Let us pray. *(Pause for silent prayer.)*

Holy and mighty God,
how quickly our song "Hosanna!"
turns to shouts of "Crucify!"
Keep us turned to you in faith, renewed in love,
filled with the hope and strength of Christ.
We face these days of exodus from death to life with him,
our redeemer and liberator from sin,
who lives and reigns with you,
one God forever and ever. Amen.

### Brief Gathering Prayer

*Leader:* Let us pray.

God who has led us in our pilgrim song,
we enter these holiest days renewed by our Lenten fast;
keep us one with Christ
through his passion and in his life everlasting,
now and forever. Amen.

### Suggested Scriptures

Isaiah 50:4–5
Philippians 2:6–8
Matthew 27:51–54

Alan J. Hommerding
Text and music © 2004, World Library Publications

# Holy Week
# The Lord's Supper, The Lord's Passion _____

## Litany

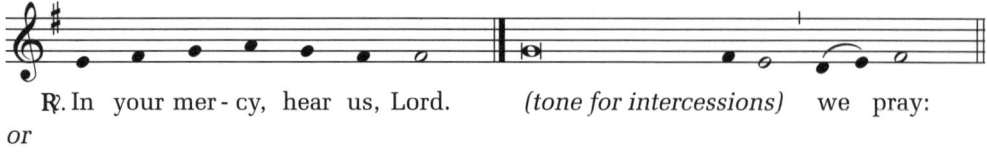

℞. In your mer-cy, hear us, Lord.     *(tone for intercessions)*     we pray:

*or*

℞. Ky-ri-e, e-le-i-son.     *(tone for intercessions)*     we pray:

*(A seasonal psalm refrain or another seasonal response may be used.)*

For the strength and desire to love one another as Christ has **loved** us,
    we pray: ℞.

That our ministry will lead all to Christ who has died, who has risen,
    who will come **a**gain, we pray: ℞.

That we might willingly kneel to wash each oth**er's** feet, we pray: ℞.

For those preparing to receive the Easter sacraments of light **and** life,
    we pray: ℞.

*(If desired, an additional invocation for particular needs may be added.)*

## Gathering Prayer

*Leader:* Let us pray. *(Pause for silent prayer.)*

Most generous God,
let us walk with Christ these last days.
As he gave himself in bread and wine,
may we give ourselves in service to the world,
following him who knelt to wash the feet of others.
following him who went forth to do your will singing a psalm.
Obedient and humble, may we remain with him in death,
and come to live with him in your boundless glory,
forever and ever. Amen.

## Brief Gathering Prayer

*Leader:* Let us pray.

In remembrance, we celebrate our Lord's Supper.
In remembrance, we give ourselves in service,
and celebrate the death of him who is our life
forever and ever. Amen.

## Suggested Scriptures

Isaiah 53:1–3
1 Corinthians 11:23–26
John 19:40–42

Alan J. Hommerding
Text and music © 2004, World Library Publications

EASTER

# Easter Day
# Christ Triumphant over Death_____

## Litany

℟. Al - le - lu-ia! Al - le-lu-ia! Al - le - lu - ia!    *(tone for intercessions)* we pray:

*\* May be sung in canon.*

*(A seasonal psalm refrain or another seasonal response may be used.)*

Alleluia! The thundering music of everlasting life roars out
of the emp**ty** tomb! we pray: ℟.

Alleluia! We have been commissioned to preach Christ crucified,
our Paschal Victim, our hope **a**risen! we pray: ℟.

Alleluia! God surrendered the only-begotten Son to death,
to ransom our souls enslaved **by** sin, we pray: ℟.

Alleluia! Christ is risen from the dead! We have been baptized into his death,
we rise to **new** life! we pray: ℟.

*(If desired, an additional invocation for particular needs may be added.)*

## Gathering Prayer

*Leader:* Let us pray. *(Pause for silent prayer.)*

God of everlasting life,
this is the day you have made
to praise you, to thank you, to bless you
for raising your Son, our brother,
Jesus Christ, first-born from the dead.
This is the day you raised us from the tomb,
born anew through the waters and Spirit of baptism.
To you we sing "Alleluia!"
now and forever. Amen.

## Brief Gathering Prayer

*Leader:* Let us pray.

Alleluia! Christ is risen indeed!
We give you thanks and praise in our music, mighty God,
for making us one in Christ,
in life everlasting,
now and forever. Amen.

## Suggested Scriptures

Acts 10:42–43
Colossians 3:1–4
Mark 16:5–7

Alan J. Hommerding
Text and music © 2004, World Library Publications

# Easter II
# Blessed Are They Who Believe_____

## Litany

R. Al - le - lu - ia! Al - le - lu - ia! Al - le - lu - ia! *(tone for intercessions)* we pray:

\* *May be sung in canon.*

*(A seasonal psalm refrain or another seasonal response may be used.)*

Alleluia! Blessed are they who gather in the name of Christ
    for prayer and break**ing** bread, we pray: R.

Alleluia! Blessed and beloved are God's children who make music
    in the Spirit **of** truth, we pray: R.

Alleluia! Blessed is the Lamb, Alpha and Omega, once dead
    but now alive **for**ever, we pray: R.

Alleluia! Blessed are they who have not seen but still believe in Christ,
    our Lord **and** God, we pray: R.

*(If desired, an additional invocation for particular needs may be added.)*

## Gathering Prayer

*Leader:* Let us pray. *(Pause for silent prayer.)*

Our Lord and our God,
bless us who believe in you.
May we behold and know your Body—
risen and glorified—here with us.
Let our joyful music and inspired song
testify in the Spirit of truth to you,
our resurrection and our life,
so that all might believe in you who live and reign,
forever and ever. Amen.

## Brief Gathering Prayer

*Leader:* Let us pray.

You come to us speaking "Peace,"
giving life in your name.
You come to us risen and glorified, wounded still.
Bless us, bring us to sing your name,
our Lord and God, forever and ever. Amen.

## Suggested Scriptures

Acts 2:42–43
1 John 5:5–6
John 20:30–31

Alan J. Hommerding
Text and music © 2004, World Library Publications

# Easter III
# Worthy Is the Lamb‗‗‗‗‗‗‗‗‗‗‗‗‗

## Litany

℞. Al - le - lu-ia! Al - le-lu-ia! Al - le - lu - ia!   *(tone for intercessions)* we pray:

\* *May be sung in canon.*

*(A seasonal psalm refrain or another seasonal response may be used.)*

Alleluia! Worthy is Christ, our Lamb. Blessing! Honor! Glo**ry**! Might!
   we pray: ℞.

Alleluia! Glorious is Christ, known to us in scripture,
   revealed to us in brea**king** bread, we pray: ℞.

Alleluia! Exalted is Christ at the right hand of God,
   pouring forth the Spirit on **our** song, we pray: ℞.

Alleluia! We are witnesses to Christ who suffered, died, and was buried;
   who lives **for**ever, we pray: ℞.

*(If desired, an additional invocation for particular needs may be added.)*

## Gathering Prayer

*Leader:* Let us pray. *(Pause for silent prayer.)*

Set our hearts aflame with your word, O Lord.
Open our lips to sing of your marvelous triumph,
our minds with understanding,
our hands in willing service
as witnesses to your name.
Lead us, with every creature in heaven and earth,
to your throne of mercy, grace, beauty, and peace,
Where we will praise you and bless you
forever and ever. Amen.

## Brief Gathering Prayer

*Leader:* Let us pray.

Stay with us, remain with us, Lord;
speak to us in your Word,
let us know you in broken bread,
keep us strong and faithful in your life everlasting,
now and forever. Amen.

## Suggested Scriptures

Acts 2:32–33
Revelation 5:11–12
Luke 24:44–48

Alan J. Hommerding
Text and music © 2004, World Library Publications

# Easter IV
# The Shepherd Is Risen

## Litany

℟. Al-le-lu-ia! Al-le-lu-ia! Al-le-lu-ia! *(tone for intercessions)* we pray:

*\* May be sung in canon.*

*(A seasonal psalm refrain or another seasonal response may be used.)*

Alleluia! Christ our Good Shepherd, Christ our Paschal Lamb
    is risen from **the** dead; we pray: ℟.

Alleluia! May we be a Church of light for the world,
    built on Christ **our** cornerstone, we pray: ℟.

Alleluia! May we, God's children, minister faithfully
    until we are revealed fully **like** Christ, we pray: ℟.

Alleluia! Let our ears hearken for the loving voice of Christ,
    **our** Shepherd, we pray: ℟.

*(If desired, an additional invocation for particular needs may be added.)*

## Gathering Prayer

*Leader:* Let us pray. *(Pause for silent prayer.)*

Shepherd of the faithful flock,
keep us mindful of your voice.
May our own voices echo your loving call
and lead others to safety in you.
Make us jubilant in new life;
let us stand firm on Christ, our cornerstone,
rejected, now resurrected, our Savior
who lives and reigns with you and the Holy Spirit,
one God forever and ever. Amen.

## Brief Gathering Prayer

*Leader:* Let us pray.

You, our Shepherd,
have named us your beloved children.
As we continue to sing "Alleluia!"
may we also heed your voice, our one living God,
forever and ever. Amen.

## Suggested Scriptures

Acts 2:38–39
1 John 3:1–2
John 10:11–12

Alan J. Hommerding
Text and music © 2004, World Library Publications

# Easter V
# All Things New in Christ_____

## Litany

℟. Al - le - lu-ia! Al - le-lu-ia! Al - le - lu - ia!     *(tone for intercessions)* we pray:

*\* May be sung in canon.*

*(A seasonal psalm refrain or another seasonal response may be used.)*

Alleluia! We are God's own people, a chosen race, a royal priesthood,
a holy nation **in** Christ, we pray: ℟.

Alleluia! May the risen Christ make us fruitful branches of the one **true** Vine,
we pray: ℟.

Alleluia! Christ calls us to sing of him, our Way, our Truth, **our** Life,
we pray: ℟.

Alleluia! May we become dwelling places for the God
who makes all **things** new, we pray: ℟.

*(If desired, an additional invocation for particular needs may be added.)*

## Gathering Prayer

*Leader:* Let us pray. *(Pause for silent prayer.)*

God who dwells among us,
in Christ we find our Way back to you,
in Christ we know the Truth of your love,
in Christ we have Life everlasting.
You have made us a chosen race,
a royal priesthood, a holy nation,
your own people sent to sing the gospel boldly,
loving as you love us,
forever and ever. Amen.

## Brief Gathering Prayer

*Leader:* Let us pray.

God among us,
who makes all things new,
continue to make us your chosen people and royal priesthood,
by our music may the world be made new in you,
now and forever. Amen.

## Suggested Scriptures

Acts 9:31
1 Peter 2:9
John 13:34–35

Alan J. Hommerding
Text and music © 2004, World Library Publications

# Easter VI
# Christ Who Sends the Spirit_____

## Litany

℞. Al - le - lu - ia! Al - le - lu - ia! Al - le - lu - ia! *(tone for intercessions)* we pray:

*\* May be sung in canon.*

*(A seasonal psalm refrain or another seasonal response may be used.)*

Alleluia! The Risen Christ bids us love one another,
    so we might receive the Ho**ly** Spirit, we pray: ℞.

Alleluia! Here we sanctify Christ—brought to life in the Spirit—
    as Lord of **our** hearts, we pray: ℞.

Alleluia! May we always minister in the way of Christ,
    the Lamb who is **our** light, we pray: ℞.

Alleluia! Let the Spirit, our Advocate, our Comforter, the Paraclete,
    rest upon us ev**ery** day, we pray: ℞.

*(If desired, an additional invocation for particular needs may be added.)*

## Gathering Prayer

*Leader:* Let us pray. *(Pause for silent prayer.)*

God whose glory is our light,
guide us to lives filled with service.
Grace us with your Holy Spirit,
who brought Christ to life.
When our work here is finished,
let our lips brim with a new song,
and bring us to your holy city to live with you
forever and ever. Amen.

## Brief Gathering Prayer

*Leader:* Let us pray.

Safeguard and strengthen us as we minister, O Lord.
May we be faithful to your commandments
and receive the Spirit, one God with you and Christ,
forever and ever. Amen.

## Suggested Scriptures

Acts 8:14–17
1 Peter 3:17–18
John 15:9–10

Alan J. Hommerding
Text and music © 2004, World Library Publications

# The Ascension of the Lord
# At the Right Hand of God_____

## Litany

℟. Al-le-lu-ia! Al-le-lu-ia! Al-le-lu-ia!     *(tone for intercessions)* we pray:

*\* May be sung in canon.*

*(A seasonal psalm refrain or another seasonal response may be used.)*

Alleluia! Clap your hands! Sing with joy! Sound the trumpet!
   Christ is **as**cended! We pray: ℟.

Alleluia! In water and the Spirit, we are witnesses of Christ
   to the ends of **the** earth, we pray: ℟.

Alleluia! The Risen Christ remains among us, one Body, many gifts,
   one in **the** Spirit, we pray: ℟.

Alleluia! May the Spirit of wisdom and revelation
   enlighten the eyes of **our** hearts, we pray: ℟.

*(If desired, an additional invocation for particular needs may be added.)*

## Gathering Prayer

*Leader:* Let us pray. *(Pause for silent prayer.)*

God of power and might,
enthroned amid the angels and saints,
your Christ is ascended to heaven,
yet remains with us and among us
through your Holy Spirit.
As we sing of his glory,
we pray that you continue to clothe us
in the light of his splendor,
forever and ever. Amen.

## Brief Gathering Prayer

*Leader:* Let us pray.

God enthroned in glory, God-among-us,
you send us into the world to spread the gospel of Christ,
keep us faithful in our mission through music,
now and forever. Amen.

## Suggested Scriptures

Acts 1:6–8
Ephesians 1:17–18
Matthew 28:18–20

Alan J. Hommerding
Text and music © 2004, World Library Publications

# Easter VII
# The Spirit and the Bride

## Litany

℞. Al - le - lu-ia! Al - le - lu-ia! Al - le - lu - ia! *(tone for intercessions)* we pray:

*\* May be sung in canon.*

*(A seasonal psalm refrain or another seasonal response may be used.)*

Alleluia! We are witnesses to Christ dead, buried, risen, ascended,
**and** glorified: we pray: ℞.

Alleluia! Let us rejoice in suffering, joined to Christ who suffered
and now lives **for**ever, we pray: ℞.

Alleluia! May our oneness in song lead all to true unity **in** Christ, we pray: ℞.

Alleluia! We, the beloved Bride, cry, "Come, Lord Jesus!"
with the voice of **the** Spirit: we pray: ℞.

*(If desired, an additional invocation for particular needs may be added.)*

## Gathering Prayer

*Leader:* Let us pray. *(Pause for silent prayer.)*

Holy and righteous God,
look on us and hear us
who are united by our faith in Christ,
our Alpha and Omega.
Make us one in the Spirit of joy,
with whom we cry *"Marana tha!"*
Care for us in suffering, lead us to your glory
with Christ our Lord, one with you and the Spirit,
forever and ever. Amen.

## Brief Gathering Prayer

*Leader:* Let us pray.

Blessed are you, Mighty God,
worthy of praise.
Keep us one in your love,
holy in your truth,
fill our voices with the voice of your Spirit,
now and forever. Amen.

## Suggested Scriptures

Acts 1:12–14
1 John 4:11–13
John 17:20–21

Alan J. Hommerding
Text and music © 2004, World Library Publications

# Pentecost
# Come, Holy Spirit

## Litany

R̷. Al - le - lu-ia! Al - le-lu-ia! Al - le - lu - ia!   *(tone for intercessions)* we pray:

*\* May be sung in canon.*

*(A seasonal psalm refrain or another seasonal response may be used.)*

Alleluia! Together in this place we wait, we implore heaven
   for the coming **of** the Spirit, we pray: R̷.

Alleluia! May the Spirit be the breath of the Church, the fire in our hearts,
   the wings of **our** song, we pray: R̷.

Alleluia! That the language of music might bring about the unity
   of the tongues **on** earth, we pray: R̷.

Alleluia! May many gifts given by one Spirit send us forth
   in witness to **the** gospel, we pray: R̷.

*(If desired, an additional invocation for particular needs may be added.)*

## Gathering Prayer

*Leader:* Let us pray. *(Pause for silent prayer.)*

Send your Spirit upon us, O God,
that we might be sent for the work of our ministry
strengthened in hope for the singing of Good News,
united by love of you and neighbor,
for the coming of your glorious reign.
We cry *"Abba!"* with Christ, in the Spirit,
forever and ever. Amen.

## Brief Gathering Prayer

*Leader:* Let us pray.

Make your Spirit burst upon us, O Lord,
in fiery tongue of witness,
in mighty breath of praise,
on soaring song of your glory,
forever and ever. Amen.

## Suggested Scriptures

Joel 3:1–3
1 Corinthians 12:12–13
John 20:21–22

Alan J. Hommerding
Text and music © 2004, World Library Publications

# DAYS OF PROCLAMATION

# Days of Proclamation
# Live in Faith_____

## Litany

℟. Hear us, O God;  send us out in your name.    *(tone for intercessions)*  we   pray:

*(A seasonal psalm refrain or another seasonal response may be used.)*

May we be living signs, sharing the loving faithfulness
  of the new covenant in **Christ**, we pray: ℟.

For steadfastness in song, for the grace to give witness to the gospel
  in every time and **place**, we pray: ℟.

For deliverance from ignorance, injustice, and indifference,
  so we may broadcast the Good News to **all**, we pray: ℟.

That we will continue to walk and serve in the ways of the faithful apostles,
  prophets, martyrs, and **saints**, we pray: ℟.

*(If desired, an additional invocation for particular needs may be added.)*

## Gathering Prayer

*Leader:* Let us pray. *(Pause for silent prayer.)*

Faithful God of our covenant,
may your presence among us today
make us shine like the stars in the sky,
promised to Abraham as a sign
of your constant love.
Let our light shine faithfully,
let our music resound brightly;
in faith, may we always give witness
to you, Father, Son, and Holy Spirit,
one God forever and ever. Amen.

## Brief Gathering Prayer

*Leader:* Let us pray.

Your faithfulness and loving-kindness, O God, fill our hearts;
may they lead and inspire our music today, our lives every day,
and bring our lives of faith, one day, to live in your glory
forever and ever. Amen.

## Suggested Scriptures

Deuteronomy 32:1–4
Romans 4:16–18
John 14:11–14

Alan J. Hommerding
Text and music © 2004, World Library Publications

# Days of Proclamation
## Live in Hope

### Litany

℞. Hear us, O God;   send us out in your name.   *(tone for intercessions)*   we   pray:

*(A seasonal psalm refrain or another seasonal response may be used.)*

May we be granted the virtue of hope, a sure and steadfast anchor
   for our **souls**, we pray: ℞.

That the Spirit, our help and consolation, will keep us tireless and confident,
   filling us with the fruits of heavenly **grace**, we pray: ℞.

For all whose hope is diminished, failing, or vanquished,
   may we reach out with the love of Christ to re**store them**, we pray: ℞.

That the music we offer the Lord and all the faithful will strengthen us
   in joyful hope, as we await his re**turn**, we pray: ℞.

*(If desired, an additional invocation for particular needs may be added.)*

### Gathering Prayer

*Leader:* Let us pray. *(Pause for silent prayer.)*

God of all times and places,
may your refreshing hope
shower down upon your people today
through the song, music, and ministry
you have granted us for the gospel.
Let us be renewed in trust,
so we may witness joyfully
until the day your Christ comes to reign
forever and ever. Amen.

### Brief Gathering Prayer

*Leader:* Let us pray.

We wait in joyful hope for the coming of Christ, O God.
Fill our song with hopefulness and all our music with joy,
so all may strive to live your will
on earth and in heaven,
forever and ever. Amen.

### Suggested Scriptures

Jeremiah 17:13–14
1 Peter 1:3–5
Matthew 12:18–21

Alan J. Hommerding
Text and music © 2004, World Library Publications

# Days of Proclamation
## Live in Love

### Litany

R̷. Hear us, O God;  send us out in your  name.    *(tone for intercessions)*  we   pray:

*(A seasonal psalm refrain or another seasonal response may be used.)*

That God's love for us in Christ will draw us closer to Christ
and to each **other**, we pray: R̷.

For the whole Church throughout the world,
for our increase in love and **unity**, we pray: R̷.

May our song for the Lord be offered with passion,
leading others to join the love-song of the **saints**, we pray: R̷.

To God, font of love; to Christ, sign of love;
to the Holy Spirit, instrument of love;
we, the Church—the home of love—lift our **voices**, we pray: R̷.

*(If desired, an additional invocation for particular needs may be added.)*

### Gathering Prayer

*Leader:* Let us pray. *(Pause for silent prayer.)*

Source and Giver of all love,
nothing can separate us from you.
Join us lovingly
in song and celebration
of that greatest love:
the passion, death, and resurrection of Christ,
who is our Savior and our God,
forever and ever. Amen.

### Brief Gathering Prayer

*Leader:* Let us pray.

We come to sing your praise,
wellspring of all creating love;
to be united in Christ, great sign of your saving love;
one in the Holy Spirit of your love for Christ and for us,
forever and ever. Amen.

### Suggested Scriptures

Song of Songs 2:1–4
Romans 8:33–37
John 13:33–35

Alan J. Hommerding
Text and music © 2004, World Library Publications

# Days of Proclamation
# Bread of Life, Blessing Cup_____

## Litany

℟. Hear us, O God; send us out in your name.    *(tone for intercessions)* we pray:

*(A seasonal psalm refrain or another seasonal response may be used.)*

Let us receive a foretaste of the celestial banquet in the Lord's Supper
and in our **song**, we pray: ℟.

That the Body of Christ will nourish us and strengthen us,
making us one for service to the **world**, we pray: ℟.

For vigor in the Blood of Christ, to endure trials and tribulations
drinking from the cup he **drank**, we pray: ℟.

With Christ, let us go forth to seek God's will, to meet our destiny
with a song on our **lips**, we pray: ℟.

*(If desired, an additional invocation for particular needs may be added.)*

## Gathering Prayer

*Leader:* Let us pray. *(Pause for silent prayer.)*

"Take and eat" is your commandment.
"Take and drink" is your commandment, too.
"Love one another" is our mandate,
"Wash each other's feet" is our example from you.
Let our music-making be strengthened
by these signs of your life for us;
let them change us, transform us,
making us your life for others,
now and forever. Amen.

## Brief Gathering Prayer

*Leader:* Let us pray.

At this, your supper, Lord, we see the forthcoming feast of heaven.
"This, my body; this my blood" is our call to follow and serve you;
let us be your presence in song for all people,
now and forever. Amen.

## Suggested Scriptures

Exodus 24:7–8
1 Corinthians 10:16–17
John 6:53–55

Alan J. Hommerding
Text and music © 2004, World Library Publications

# Days of Proclamation
# Forgive As We Forgive

## Litany

℞. Hear us, O God;   send us out in your name.      *(tone for intercessions)*   we   pray:

*(A seasonal psalm refrain or another seasonal response may be used.)*

Let us follow Christ to the cross, where earth and heaven are re**conciled**,
    we pray: ℞.

That our music will open hearts to God's grace, hasten forgiveness,
    strengthen the work of **healing**, we pray: ℞.

For the courage to beseech God to forgive us as we forgive oth**ers**,
    we pray: ℞.

May the Good News of forgiveness and reconciliation be embraced
    in our tender **song**, we pray: ℞.

*(If desired, an additional invocation for particular needs may be added.)*

## Gathering Prayer

*Leader:* Let us pray. *(Pause for silent prayer.)*

Loving, forgiving, saving Lord,
you know our failings,
yet you love us still;
we turn from you,
but you rush to greet us in forgiveness.
Let our song today begin your mercy,
and emulate heaven's joy at our reconciliation.
Heal us, forgive us as we forgive others,
now and forever. Amen.

## Brief Gathering Prayer

*Leader:* Let us pray.

Merciful God, look on our faithfulness and not our sins,
let our ministry in music imitate the forgiving embrace of Christ,
who redeems us, who bestows your Holy Spirit on us,
forever and ever. Amen.

## Suggested Scriptures

Jeremiah 31:33–34
Ephesians 1:3–8
Luke 17:3–4

Alan J. Hommerding
Text and music © 2004, World Library Publications

# Days of Proclamation
# Hearts Filled with Gratitude_____

## Litany

℞. Hear us, O God; send us out in your name.    *(tone for intercessions)* we pray:
*(A seasonal psalm refrain or another seasonal response may be used.)*

For the beauty and bounty of creation; may our gratitude lead us to be wiser,
    prudent stewards of the **earth**, we pray: ℞.

For all peoples of the world, beloved children of God; may we find in their
    faces a glimpse of the infinite love of the **Lord**, we pray: ℞.

For the abundant riches of our faith; may thankful hearts lead us again and
    again to the table of the Lord's Word, Bread, and **Cup**, we pray: ℞.

For every gift, for the gifts and talents of our music-making;
    may our grateful lives shine and sing in witness to **Christ**, we pray: ℞.

*(If desired, an additional invocation for particular needs may be added.)*

## Gathering Prayer

*Leader:* Let us pray. *(Pause for silent prayer.)*

God most generous,
you give us our daily bread
and the bread of life.
May these strengthen us to serve you
and minister to the people
you have called into the light of Christ.
Let us consecrate every gift of music
gratefully to your glory,
forever and ever. Amen.

## Brief Gathering Prayer

*Leader:* Let us pray.

You, O Lord, who give and forgive,
are the source of our gratitude.
May our prayer today in music lead others to give you thanks
and to praise you, one, true, and living God,
now and forever. Amen.

## Suggested Scriptures

Joel 2:21–23
Philippians 4:8–9
Matthew 6:31–33

Alan J. Hommerding
Text and music © 2004, World Library Publications

# Days of Proclamation
# In the Sight of the Angels

## Litany

℟. Hear us, O God; send us out in your name.   *(tone for intercessions)* we   pray:

*(A seasonal psalm refrain or another seasonal response may be used.)*

With the angels who announced the Savior's coming, who sang "Gloria!"
  at his birth, who sat in the silence of the empty **tomb**, we pray: ℟.

For lives that fulfill the call of our baptism to be herald messengers
  of glad **tidings**, we pray: ℟.

May we remember, in times of trial, fear, or distress,
  that God's angels have been given charge o**ver us**, we pray: ℟.

That the song of our earthly ministry will inspire us and lead us
  to join the voices of the angel **choirs**, we pray: ℟.

*(If desired, an additional invocation for particular needs may be added.)*

## Gathering Prayer

*Leader:* Let us pray. *(Pause for silent prayer.)*

Lord of the heavenly hosts,
mightier than cherubim and seraphim,
you bid your angel messengers
guard us and guide us.
Let us share their joy when sinners return,
and may our music-making today
join with theirs to announce your glory,
with your Christ and the Spirit,
one God forever and ever. Amen.

## Brief Gathering Prayer

*Leader:* Let us pray.

Rank upon rank, choir upon choir of angels worship you, Lord.
They bore your Good News in Christ
from his annunciation to his ascension.
May we, too, be heralds of the gospel in our music,
now and forever. Amen.

## Suggested Scriptures

Isaiah 6:1–3
1 Timothy 3:16
John 20:11–13

# Days of Proclamation
# The Way, the Truth, the Life_____

## Litany

℟. Hear us, O God; send us out in your name.   *(tone for intercessions)*  we   pray:
*(A seasonal psalm refrain or another seasonal response may be used.)*

Christ, you are the Way to salvation; walk with your faithful pilgrims,
   singing with us on our **journey**, we pray: ℟.

Christ, you are the Truth that fills our prayer in song;
   guide us to seek and find your truth in **love**, we pray: ℟.

Christ, you are the Life everlasting, the glory that angels and saints sing;
   unite our song with **theirs**, we pray: ℟.

Our Way, our Truth, our Life, show us the path to heaven,
   lead our tongues to what is right, sustain us to **serve**: we pray: ℟.

*(If desired, an additional invocation for particular needs may be added.)*

## Gathering Prayer

*Leader:* Let us pray. *(Pause for silent prayer.)*

God of eternal Glory,
we behold you in Jesus Christ,
our Way, our Truth, our Life.
He is with us through your Spirit;
we know him, and so we know you.
Send your Spirit in tongues of flame
to guide our tongues to sing and exalt you
in our music here and hereafter,
forever and forever. Amen.

## Brief Gathering Prayer

*Leader:* Let us pray.

Loving Father of Jesus Christ,
our Way, Truth, and Life,
may Christ fill our music
to lead us, teach us, create us anew.
Send your Spirit to sing among us,
now and forever. Amen.

## Suggested Scriptures

Isaiah 28:16–17
Ephesians 2:17–19
John 14:5–7

Alan J. Hommerding
Text and music © 2004, World Library Publications

# Days of Proclamation
# Praise the Trinity

## Litany

R̸. God Most High,* hear and an-swer us.   *(tone for intercessions)*   we pray:

*\* Other invocations may be used: God of love, God our strength, Saving God.*

*(A seasonal psalm refrain or another seasonal response may be used.)*

We praise you, God our Father, for saving us in Christ,
for sustaining us **through** your Spirit, we pray: R̸.

We praise you, Jesus Christ our Lord, for your life, passion, death,
and resurrection, until you **come** in glory, we pray: R̸.

We praise you, Holy Spirit, in whom we are born anew,
with whom we cry out *"Marana tha!"* we pray: R̸.

We praise you, Most Holy Trinity, with every breath,
with every note of our song, Father, Son, and **Ho**ly Spirit, we pray: R̸.

*(If desired, an additional invocation for particular needs may be added.)*

## Gathering Prayer

*Leader:* Let us pray. *(Pause for silent prayer.)*

We pray to you, One God in Three Persons,
who fashioned us in your own image,
who took on our human flesh to save us,
who continues to grace and guide the Church.
May the love in which you dwell
surround our ministry to your people;
let your delight in one another, O Three-in-One,
fill our song with delight in you,
one God, forever and ever. Amen.

## Brief Gathering Prayer

*Leader:* Let us pray.

We praise you today and every day,
Father, Son, and Holy Spirit.
Bless our ministry of music with your great and holy name,
we pray to you, our one, true, and living God,
forever and ever. Amen.

## Suggested Scriptures

Deuteronomy 6:3–5
2 Corinthians 13:11–13
Matthew 28:17–20

Alan J. Hommerding
Text and music © 2004, World Library Publications

# Days of Proclamation
# The Mother of God_____

## Litany

℟. God Most High,*   hear and an-swer us.   *(tone for intercessions)*   we   pray:

\* *Other invocations may be used: God of love, God our strength, Saving God.*

*(A seasonal psalm refrain or another seasonal response may be used.)*

That Mary's "Let it be done" will inspire us to be open to the **will** of God,
we pray: ℟.

That the grace of the Holy Spirit might overshadow us,
making the Word flesh in **our** own lives, we pray: ℟.

For the desire to hold the mysteries of Christ **in** our hearts, we pray: ℟.

That we may follow the Son of Mary, walking with her as faithful disciples,
even to the foot **of** the cross, we pray: ℟.

*(If desired, an additional invocation for particular needs may be added.)*

## Gathering Prayer

*Leader:* Let us pray. *(Pause for silent prayer.)*

Our souls rejoice in you, God our Savior.
As you once sent your angel to a young girl in Galilee,
visit us, speak to us, be here with us now.
We follow the example of Christ—"Your will be done"—
when we echo his mother—"Let it be done to me as you say."
May our ministry lead others to know you,
God-among-us, through the power of the Spirit,
one God, forever and ever. Amen.

## Brief Gathering Prayer

*Leader:* Let us pray.

Your will be done on earth as in heaven, O Lord.
May we, like Mary, joyfully answer "Yes" to your call,
and with her come to live with you,
forever and ever. Amen.

## Suggested Scriptures

Zephaniah 3:14–15
Galatians 4:4–6
Luke 11:27–28

Alan J. Hommerding
Text and music © 2004, World Library Publications

# Days of Proclamation
# The Cloud of Witnesses_____

## Litany

℞. God Most High,* hear and an-swer us. *(tone for intercessions)* we pray:

*\* Other invocations may be used: God of love, God our strength, Saving God.*

*(A seasonal psalm refrain or another seasonal response may be used.)*

That the song of our worship on earth will join us to the worship
of the celestial choir at the throne **of** the Lamb; we pray: ℞.

That the Spirit will guide us in the mystic union of the holy ones of heaven
and the saints we **know** on earth, we pray: ℞.

For all who work for justice, equality, and peace; may we see in their work
the coming of the **reign** of God, we pray: ℞.

For the strength of our own witness; may the example of our lives
and our elation in music lead others **to** God's will, we pray: ℞.

*(If desired, an additional invocation for particular needs may be added.)*

## Gathering Prayer

*Leader:* Let us pray. *(Pause for silent prayer.)*

God enthroned in heavenly splendor,
you are surrounded by the saints, who endlessly sing
"Blessing! Honor! Glory! Wisdom! Thanks! Praise! "
Let us join our voices to their hymn,
filling the world with their witness and ours,
so all may know your holy presence.
We sing to you, Father, Son, and Spirit,
now and forever. Amen.

## Brief Gathering Prayer

*Leader:* Let us pray.

Lord of light eternal,
you call countless numbers of your children "blessed."
May our hearts and voices unite with theirs in a hymn of praise.
Make us witnesses of your saving power
through Christ, in the Spirit,
forever and ever. Amen.

## Suggested Scriptures

Wisdom 3:1–3
Hebrews 12:1–2
Matthew 11:25–27

Alan J. Hommerding
Text and music © 2004, World Library Publications

# Days of Proclamation
# Christ Will Come Again

## Litany

℟. God Most High,*   hear and an-swer us.   *(tone for intercessions)*   we   pray:

*\* Other invocations may be used: God of love, God our strength, Saving God.*

*(A seasonal psalm refrain or another seasonal response may be used.)*

Christ has died! On his cross and in his tomb we find our humanity,
    our victory, **and** our peace, we pray: ℟.

Christ is risen! Raised from the dead, we know our destiny, our delight,
    **and** our hope, we pray: ℟.

Christ will come again! We wait in joyful expectation for his sovereignty,
    our bliss, **and** our glory, we pray: ℟.

Christ, come to us in our song, in our ministry, in every daily action
    for beauty, chari**ty**, and justice, we pray: ℟.

*(If desired, an additional invocation for particular needs may be added.)*

## Gathering Prayer

*Leader:* Let us pray. *(Pause for silent prayer.)*

Almighty, eternal God,
your Christ came in our human flesh
so you could sing with your creation;
your Christ came to suffer, die, and rise again
so we would know our future glory.
May our music, our lives, ring out as signs
of his reign among us, his reign still to come,
with you and the Spirit,
one God forever and forever. Amen.

## Brief Gathering Prayer

*Leader:* Let us pray.

Christ, you are with us through the Spirit,
yet still hidden from our sight.
Come to us and be revealed through our music today.
May all we do be a sign of your reign to come,
forever and ever. Amen.

## Suggested Scriptures

Daniel 7:13–14
James 5:7–8
Mark 13:24

Alan J. Hommerding
Text and music © 2004, World Library Publications

# Ministry Occasions

# Ministry Occasions
# A First Rehearsal

## Litany

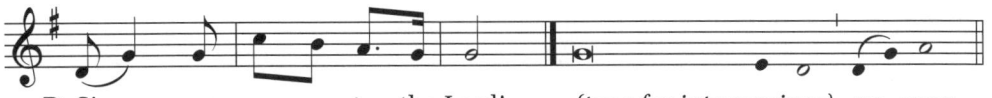

℟. Sing a new song to the Lord! *(tone for intercessions)* we pray:

*(A seasonal psalm refrain or another seasonal response may be used.)*

For blessings on all who minister by making music
  for the glory **of** God, we pray: ℟.

For the blessing, guidance, and wisdom of the Spirit
  in all our work, prayer, **and** play, we pray: ℟.

For the life of this community, for renewed dedication
  to share the **Good** News, we pray: ℟.

That God will restore and refresh our own lives
  and the lives we touch **with** music, we pray: ℟.

*(If desired, an additional invocation for particular needs may be added.)*

## Gathering Prayer

*Leader:* Let us pray. *(Pause for silent prayer.)*

Lord our God,
you are the source of all music,
the source of every gift and talent we have.
May we consecrate our lives to you,
fulfilling the command of Christ to teach all nations.
Let every sound we make be dedicated to leading souls to you,
causing us to look to that day
when we join around your throne
in a glorious eternal psalm, giving you praise
forever and ever. Amen.

## Brief Gathering Prayer

*Leader:* Let us pray.

God of beauty and joy,
you graced Miriam's Exodus canticle;
you guided David's hand upon the harp.
Grace us and guide us now.
Fill us with your praise,
you who live and reign forever and ever. Amen.

## Suggested Scriptures

Deuteronomy 31:19–22
Colossians 3:15–17
John 15:12–16

Alan J. Hommerding
Text and music © 2004, World Library Publications

# Ministry Occasions
# A Final Rehearsal_____

### Litany

℞. Sing a new song to the Lord! *(tone for intercessions)* we pray:

*(A seasonal psalm refrain or another seasonal response may be used.)*

In thankful praise for the grace and blessings we have received
 in our **music**making, we pray: ℞.

That the saving work of God will live on in our hearts, hands, **and** voices,
 we pray: ℞.

For our safety and well-being as we go forth from this place,
 and for our happy **re**turn, we pray: ℞.

For lives renewed and refreshed for the work **of** ministry, we pray: ℞.

*(If desired, an additional invocation for particular needs may be added.)*

### Gathering Prayer

*Leader:* Let us pray. *(Pause for silent prayer.)*

Lord our God,
in your name we have gathered to give you praise.
We thank you for the music we have made for your glory.
Continue to bless us as we go our separate ways.
Hold us in your care; make us true disciples of Christ.
Keep your Spirit alive in our hearts.
May your song always be on our lips
until that day we are united again,
one in voice, one in the timeless canticle of heaven,
forever and ever. Amen.

### Brief Gathering Prayer

*Leader:* Let us pray.

Divine Maker of all music,
we have praised you in your temple.
May we now join with all that has life and breath,
with every nation on earth,
to sustain the song of your loving-kindness,
our one God, forever and ever. Amen.

### Suggested Scriptures

1 Chronicles 16:31–32
Philippians 4:8–9
Matthew 28:19–20

Alan J. Hommerding
Text and music © 2004, World Library Publications

# Ministry Occasions
# Welcoming a New Music Minister_____

## Litany

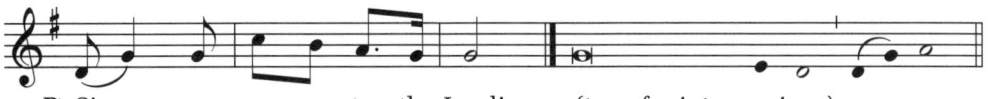

℞. Sing a new song to the Lord! *(tone for intercessions)* we pray:

*(A seasonal psalm refrain or another seasonal response may be used.)*

For joyful hearts, ready to shout the praises of **the** Lord, we pray: ℞.

For the unceasing power and presence of the Spirit,
who makes all **things** new, we pray: ℞.

For the welcoming, generous embrace of Jesus Christ, God-among-us,
in **new** friendships, we pray: ℞.

That our music-making will bring us and others closer **in** Christ, we pray: ℞.

*(If desired, an additional invocation for particular needs may be added.)*

## Prayer of Blessing

*Leader:* Let us pray.

*(All extend hands in blessing, or lay hands on the new music minister.)*

Bless *[N.]* our *sister/brother* with strength and hope,
now and forever. Amen.

Let us all grow in faith, hope, love, and unity with *her/him*,
now and forever. Amen.

May the blessing of almighty God,
Father, Son, ✠ and Holy Spirit,
remain with us, now and forever. Amen.

*(A Sign of Peace may be exchanged, or:)*

## Prayer

*Leader:* Let us pray. *(Pause for silent prayer.)*

Lord, you lead us to sing your song
even in a foreign place.
We are strangers no longer, one in faith,
one through the gift of music.
May we grow in unity through Christ,
in the Holy Spirit, now and forever. Amen.

## Suggested Scriptures

Genesis 18:1–5
Acts 18:25–27
Luke 10:38–42

Alan J. Hommerding
Text and music © 2004, World Library Publications

# Ministry Occasions
# Departure of a Music Minister_____

## Litany

℟. Sing a new song to the Lord! *(tone for intercessions)* we pray:

*(A seasonal psalm refrain or another seasonal response may be used.)*

For all messengers of the gospel of peace, for all who sing of **God's** glory,
we pray: ℟.

For a continued outpouring of the Spirit's grace as we say our **fare**well,
we pray: ℟.

With thankfulness for time and talent shared, in gratitude for Christ
revealed in laughter **and** tears, we pray: ℟.

That joy will be restored to saddened hearts as we grow in our oneness
in **the** Lord, we pray: ℟.

*(If desired, an additional invocation for particular needs may be added.)*

## Prayer of Blessing

*Leader:* Let us pray.

*(All extend hands in blessing, or lay hands on the departing minister.)*

Bless *[N.]* our *sister/brother* with joyful peace,
now and forever. Amen.

Watch over, protect, and guide *her/him*,
now and forever. Amen.

May the blessing of almighty God,
Father, Son, ✠ and Holy Spirit,
remain with us, now and forever. Amen.

*(A Sign of Peace may be exchanged, or:)*

## Prayer

*Leader:* Let us pray. *(Pause for silent prayer.)*

God in whom we live, move and have our being,
you brought Israel safely to a new home.
May the gift of music bring us to our home in you,
now and forever. Amen.

## Suggested Scriptures

Numbers 6:22–27
2 Timothy 4:1–2
Luke 9:1–6

Alan J. Hommerding
Text and music © 2004, World Library Publications

# Ministry Occasions
# Death of a Music Minister_____

## Litany

℞. Sing a new song to the Lord!     *(tone for intercessions)* we pray:

*(A seasonal psalm refrain or another seasonal response may be used.)*

We remember, O Lord, our *sister/brother [N.],* called from us
     to join the song that is ev**er** new, we pray: ℞.

For those who sing your praises on earth; may we look forward
     to uniting with *N.* once again when the last trum**pet** sounds, we pray: ℞.

For all who grieve the passing of *N.;* may those who mourn be blessed,
     may your song be **our** strength, we pray: ℞.

We remember the faithful departed who have made music for your glory;
     may their memory make the choirs of paradise seem **like** home, we pray: ℞.

*(If desired, an additional invocation for particular needs may be added.)*

## Gathering Prayer

*Leader:* Let us pray. *(Pause for silent prayer.)*

God of the living and the dead,
as we sing our farewell to our *sister/brother [N.],*
send the choirs of paradise
to guide *her/him* to your throne in song.
Grant *her/him* eternal rest, and walk with us in our grief.
Remember us in your kingdom,
now and forever. Amen.

## Brief Gathering Prayer

*Leader:* Let us pray.

Lord of life,
your angel choirs lead us to our heavenly home.
May they welcome our *sister/brother [N.]* with songs of rejoicing.
Grant us joy in the midst of mourning,
in the resurrection of Christ,
now and forever. Amen.

## Suggested Scriptures

Isaiah 25:7–9
1 Corinthians 15:51–55
Matthew 11:28–30

Alan J. Hommerding
Text and music © 2004, World Library Publications

# Ministry Occasions
# Ecumenical Gatherings of Musicians_____

### Litany

℟. Sing a new song to the Lord! *(tone for intercessions)* we pray:

*(A seasonal psalm refrain or another seasonal response may be used.)*

With thanks to God Almighty for the gift of music, for its beauty and power,
   for its life in **our** worship, we pray: ℟.

That our music may open hearts for reconciliation's pursuit,
   for the mission of unity **in** Christ, we pray: ℟.

For the presence of the Spirit among us, inspiring every word and note,
   blowing all places as the breath of **the** Church, we pray: ℟.

May we all grow in faith, hope, and love this day; may God bless
   all music-makers in the service of prayer **and** praise, we pray: ℟.

*(If desired, an additional invocation for particular needs may be added.)*

### Gathering Prayer

*Leader:* Let us pray. *(Pause for silent prayer.)*

God of might and majesty,
Christ of healing and peace,
Spirit of joy and beauty,
let your face shine upon us today
as we gather to make music
for the glory of your name.
Through us, may your message
resound to the ends of the earth,
now and forever. Amen.

### Brief Gathering Prayer

*Leader:* Let us pray.

To you alone our praise and worship is due, O God.
Make your presence known among us today in our music.
Let us find your image in all your children,
both now and forever. Amen.

### Suggested Scriptures

2 Chronicles 29:25–27
Colossians 3:15–17
John 17:18–21

Alan J. Hommerding
Text and music © 2004, World Library Publications

# Ministry Occasions
# Before a Concert, Tour, or Recording _____

## Litany

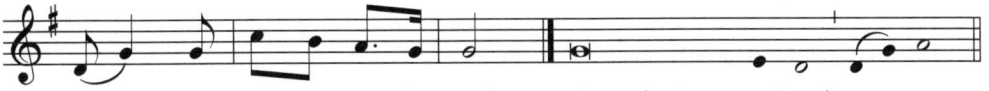

℞. Sing a new song to the Lord! *(tone for intercessions)* we pray:

*(A seasonal psalm refrain or another seasonal response may be used.)*

That the music we make will bring others to follow the Good News
of salvation **in** Christ, we pray: ℞.

With thanks to the Holy Spirit who inspired the authors and composers
whose music **we** offer, we pray: ℞.

For all who will listen and hear us; may their ears be opened
to the Word **of** life, we pray: ℞.

*Before a Concert:*

For calm and steadfast spirits, peaceful in the strength of the gospel **we** sing,
we pray: ℞.

*Before a Tour:*

For our safety and the safety of all travelers, may God watch over us
as faithful **dis**ciples, we pray: ℞.

*Before a Recording:*

For patient and cheerful hearts, continuing to be watchful and alert
to proclaim **the** gospel, we pray: ℞.

## Gathering Prayer

*Leader:* Let us pray. *(Pause for silent prayer.)*

You are enthroned in majesty amid the choirs of paradise, O God;
may the beauty of our music and our joy in praising you
allow the splendor of your presence to shine for all.
Help us to remain your faithful servants in the work of the gospel,
now and forever. Amen.

## Brief Gathering Prayer

*Leader:* Let us pray.

We, your servants, come before you, O Lord our God,
asking you to be with us as we make music to exalt you.
Bless us, keep us strong and devoted to our ministry,
now and forever. Amen.

## Suggested Scriptures

Numbers 6:22–26
1 Corinthians 14:15–16
John 1:35–37

Alan J. Hommerding
Text and music © 2004, World Library Publications

# Ministry Occasions
# St. Cecilia, Patron of Musicians_____

## Litany

℟. Sing a new song to the Lord!   *(tone for intercessions)* we pray:

*(A seasonal psalm refrain or another seasonal response may be used.)*

Let us join all that has life and breath to raise a joyful sound **to** God,
     we pray: ℟.

That the witness of our music will lead others to Christ
     and **the** gospel, we pray: ℟.

That every gift and talent will be consecrated to the **Good** News, we pray: ℟.

That the Spirit's hopeful, joyful peace will sing in our hearts
     and through **our** lives, we pray: ℟.

*(If desired, an additional invocation for particular needs may be added.)*

## Gathering Prayer

*Leader:* Let us pray. *(Pause for silent prayer.)*

God of saints and angels,
we raise our voices with Cecilia and the heavenly host.
May our harmonies inspire us
to work for unity and accord in the world,
our song lead us to yearn for your reign
of justice, joy, beauty, and peace.
Keep us faithful in your service.
Consecrate our gift of music for the gospel,
until that day we join the celestial choir
around your throne of glory.
*Cantate!* We sing! *Te Deum!* To you, Lord,
forever and ever. Amen.

## Brief Gathering Prayer

*Leader:* Let us pray.

With the music of voices and instruments we praise you, O God.
Inspire us on this feast and every day
until we join Saint Cecilia and the choirs of heaven,
one in praise around your throne
forever and ever. Amen.

## Suggested Scriptures

Zechariah 2:10–11
Revelation 5:9–10
John 1:14–17

Alan J. Hommerding
Text and music © 2004, World Library Publications

# Scripture Index